THE
PRODIGAL
SON

THE
PRODIGAL
SON

An Astonishing Study of the Parable Jesus
Told to Unveil God's Grace for You

STUDY GUIDE
GROUPS / INDIVIDUALS
FIVE SESSIONS

JOHN MACARTHUR

NELSON
BOOKS
An Imprint of Thomas Nelson

The Prodigal Son Study Guide
© 2016 John MacArthur

Published in Nashville, Tennessee, by Nelson Books, an imprint of Thomas Nelson. Nelson Books and Thomas Nelson are registered trademarks of HarperCollins Christian Publishing, Inc.

"Unleashing God's Truth, One Verse at a Time"" is a trademark of Grace to You. All rights reserved.

Thomas Nelson titles may be purchased in bulk for educational, business, fundraising, or sales promotional use. For information, please e-mail SpecialMarkets@ThomasNelson.com.

Scripture quotations are taken from *The New King James Version.* © 1982 by Thomas Nelson. Used by permission. All rights reserved.

ISBN 978-0-310-08123-4

First Printing August 2016 / Printed in the United States of America

CONTENTS

HOW TO USE THIS GUIDE

Of all Jesus' parables, the prodigal son is the most richly detailed, powerfully dramatic, and intensely personal. It's full of emotion—ranging from sadness, to triumph, to a sense of shock, and finally to an unsettling wish for more closure. The characters are familiar, so it's easy for us to identify with the prodigal, to feel the father's grief, and yet still (in some degree) sympathize with the elder brother—all at the same time.

The story is memorable on many levels, not the least of which is the gritty imagery that Jesus invokes throughout the parable. For instance, consider Jesus' description of the prodigal son being so desperately hungry that he was willing to eat husks scavenged from the pigs. This would have graphically depicted the son's youthful dissolution in a way that was unspeakably revolting to Jesus' Jewish audience.

In this study, you will delve into the Bible to explore the depths of this amazing story. In each session, expect an opening icebreaker-type question, a short Bible study, and then some time with John MacArthur on the video. Following the video, you will take some time to discuss what you learned and talk through some of the key points with your group. (Note that even though there are many questions provided, you do not need to use them all. Your leader will focus on the ones that resonate most with your group and guide you from there.)

The final component of each session is called "Opening Up to the Parable." In this part of the study, your group will engage in a more hands-on type of exercise intended to move the message of the session from your head to your heart. Think of this time as an answer to the question, "What am I supposed to *do* with this message?" The hope is that this section will serve as a place where the big ideas of *The Prodigal Son* take on some flesh-and-blood reality.

Following your group time, there will be three more opportunities for you to engage the content of the study during the week. This between-sessions personal study is arranged into three parts: (1) an *action*-oriented exercise, which will help you incorporate the principles of the study into your daily life; (2) a *contemplation*-oriented exercise, which will help you focus on the key Scripture of the session; and (3) a *reflection*-oriented exercise, which will enable you to go deeper into the topic and explore the concepts in the accompanying *The Prodigal Son* book.

Beginning in session 2, there will be time before the video for you to check in about the previous week's activities and process your experiences as a group. However, don't worry if you could not do an activity one week or if you are just joining the study. You will gain a lot of insights into Jesus' parables—in particular the parable of the prodigal son—just by listening to what others have learned during their time with the Word.

This study will open your eyes to many facets of the parable of the prodigal son that you likely have not considered before. However, if you want to get the most out of your experience, keep the following in mind: First, remember that the real growth in this study will happen *during your group time.* This is where you will process the content of the message, ask questions, and learn from others, so take advantage of this time.

Second, note that while small groups can be a deeply rewarding time of intimacy and friendship, they can also be a vehicle that can create problems and tensions between people. For this reason, work to make your group a "safe place" for people. This means being honest about your thoughts and feelings as well as listening carefully to everyone else's opinion.

Third, be sure to resist the temptation to "fix" a problem that someone might be having or shut down someone whose opinion doesn't completely match your own. You want to make your small group a place where people feel open to talk about God and share their feelings, so try to foster this type of environment whenever possible.

Finally, be sure to keep everything your group shares confidential. All this will foster a rewarding sense of community in your group and give God's Spirit some space to challenge and transform you to become more like the father in this remarkable tale.

Note: If you are a leader, you'll find additional instructions and resources for leading your small group through this study at the back of the guide. Some of the activities in the "Opening Up to the Parable" section require additional materials and setup, so be sure you read this over beforehand in order to be prepared.

PARABLES

Unveiling God's Truth through Stories

The Prodigal Son parable is without dispute one of the finest examples of storytelling ever—with its penetrating appeal to hearers' emotions and imaginations; its succinct, tightly crafted form; and its powerful and personally engaging message.

JOHN MACARTHUR

Imagine that you are being criticized for doing some-thing that you know is right—something not just okay but deeply good. How do you respond to this criticism? You might feel hurt, angry, or defensive. You might be tempted to lash out at your critics or to retreat and avoid the conflict. Or, if you're Jesus, you might calmly tell several brief stories that express why you're doing what you're doing.

Jesus didn't tell these stories because He was incapable of carrying on a direct debate. In fact, He had previously tried talking to His critics using plain language. But that had only served to inflame them so much that they plot-ted His death long before the time for His self-sacrifice was ripe. So Jesus resorted to speaking to His opponents in stories, where the point was clear to anyone who took the trouble to think them through.

This is the setting in which Jesus told one of His most famous stories: the parable of the prodigal son.

Opening the Study

Go around the group and invite everyone to intro-duce himself or herself, and then answer the following questions:

- When you were in high school, how did you see yourself—as one of the "good" kids, the "bad" kids, or somewhere in between? Why?

- What is one thing you did that illustrates who you were at that time?

Reading the Word

Read Luke 15 aloud in the group. (You might have a different person read each paragraph.) If you've read these parables before, try to open yourself to them and their context with fresh eyes and a receptive heart. Let the wonder of God's grace fill you through these simple but powerful words.

¹ Then all the tax collectors and the sinners drew near to Him to hear Him. ² And the Pharisees and scribes complained, saying, "This Man receives sinners and eats with them." ³ So He spoke this parable to them, saying:

⁴ "What man of you, having a hundred sheep, if he loses one of them, does not leave the ninety-nine in the wilderness, and go after the one which is lost until he finds it? ⁵ And when he has found it, he lays it on his shoulders, rejoicing. ⁶ And when he comes home, he calls together his friends and neighbors, saying to them, 'Rejoice with me, for I have found my sheep which was lost!' ⁷ I say to you that likewise there will be more joy in heaven over one sinner who repents than over ninety-nine just persons who need no repentance.

⁸ "Or what woman, having ten silver coins, if she loses one coin, does not light a lamp, sweep the house, and search carefully until she finds it? ⁹ And when she has found it, she calls her friends and neighbors together, saying, 'Rejoice with me, for I have found the piece which I lost!' ¹⁰ Likewise, I say to you, there is joy in the presence of the angels of God over one sinner who repents."

[11] Then He said: "A certain man had two sons. [12] And the younger of them said to his father, 'Father, give me the portion of goods that falls to me.' So he divided to them his livelihood. [13] And not many days after, the younger son gathered all together, journeyed to a far country, and there wasted his possessions with prodigal living. [14] But when he had spent all, there arose a severe famine in that land, and he began to be in want. [15] Then he went and joined himself to a citizen of that country, and he sent him into his fields to feed swine. [16] And he would gladly have filled his stomach with the pods that the swine ate, and no one gave him anything.

[17] "But when he came to himself, he said, 'How many of my father's hired servants have bread enough and to spare, and I perish with hunger! [18] I will arise and go to my father, and will say to him, "Father, I have sinned against heaven and before you, [19] and I am no longer worthy to be called your son. Make me like one of your hired servants."'

[20] "And he arose and came to his father. But when he was still a great way off, his father saw him and had compassion, and ran and fell on his neck and kissed him. [21] And the son said to him, 'Father, I have sinned against heaven and in your sight, and am no longer worthy to be called your son.'

[22] "But the father said to his servants, 'Bring out the best robe and put it on him, and put a ring on his hand and sandals on his feet. [23] And bring the fatted calf here and kill it, and let us eat and be merry; [24] for this my son was dead and is alive again; he was lost and is found.' And they began to be merry.

[25] *"Now his older son was in the field. And as he came and drew near to the house, he heard music and dancing. [26] So he called one of the servants and asked what these things meant. [27] And he said to him, 'Your brother has come, and because he has received him safe and sound, your father has killed the fatted calf.'*

[28] *"But he was angry and would not go in. Therefore his father came out and pleaded with him. [29] So he answered and said to his father, 'Lo, these many years I have been serving you; I never transgressed your commandment at any time; and yet you never gave me a young goat, that I might make merry with my friends. [30] But as soon as this son of yours came, who has devoured your livelihood with harlots, you killed the fatted calf for him.'*

[31] *"And he said to him, 'Son, you are always with me, and all that I have is yours. [32] It was right that we should make merry and be glad, for your brother was dead and is alive again, and was lost and is found.'"*

Turn to the person next to you and take turns sharing your answers to the following questions:

- What was one thing that stood out to you from the reading? In what ways did that represent a new insight?

- What do verses 1 and 2 tell you about the context in which Jesus told the three stories? Who was His audience? Why did He tell the stories?

- In the story of the lost sheep (verses 4–7), do you identify more with the one lost sheep or the ninety-nine that didn't go astray? Why?

Watching the Video

Play the video teaching segment for session 1. As you watch, use the following outline to record any thoughts or concepts that stand out to you.

NOTES

The word *parable* comes from a Greek term that means to lay something alongside. In a parable, Jesus put a story alongside a spiritual truth to make that spiritual truth clear.

All parables have one main idea. The main idea in this parable is that the Pharisees and scribes—the religious leaders of Israel who thought they knew and represented God—had no knowledge of the mind or heart of God. Jesus, who is God, was preaching the gospel to the lowlifes of his day, and they repented of their sin. The leaders of Israel were irate about this.

God rejoices in the repentance of sinners, not in the self-righteousness of hypocrites.

Jesus told the three stories in Luke 15 out of mercy. He told them to the wrongdoing scribes and Pharisees as a warning that they were out of touch with God.

The prodigal son was the worst sinner that Jesus could have invented. He was outrageous, but in the end he finds reconciliation with the father.

The reconciling father is Jesus Christ, who receives the most extreme sinner.

The older brother is the Pharisees and the scribes, who were angry at the father's forgiveness. These religious hypocrites thought they were earning their way into heaven and had no concept of grace.

There are only two possibilities: either we seek to receive salvation by our own righteous deeds or we go to God repentant, recognizing our sin, and receive the grace of a reconciling Father.

If we are depending on our works to earn our way into God's favor, it won't happen. Salvation is a gift of grace that comes when we repent, because Christ has paid the penalty for our sin.

Group Discussion

Take a few minutes with your group members to discuss what you just watched and explore these concepts in Scripture.

1. After watching the video, what is one question you have that you would like to share with the group?

2. The main "enemies" of Jesus' ministry were the scribes and Pharisees. What did the scribes and Pharisees not understand about Jesus' mission?

3. What are some adjectives that would describe the Pharisees and scribes?

4. What does it say about God that there's a party in heaven each time someone repents?

5. Who do you currently identify with most in the story of the prodigal son: the younger son, the older son, or the father? Why?

6. What are some modern-day settings where you might encounter people like the scribes and the Pharisees? What characteristics do those people display?

7. What is *self-righteousness*? How can you guard against it in your own life?

Opening Up to the Parable

For this activity, each participant will need a blank piece of paper and a pen. The group leader will also need an empty pot or bowl.

The scribes and Pharisees viewed certain types of people as unworthy of God's favor, and they were angry when those people showed signs of repentance. In their eyes, the tax collectors and other notorious sinners shouldn't and couldn't be forgiven. Is there any person or type of person (a religious group, political group, ethnic group, a criminal) that you see as unforgivable? Or a person you've given up praying about for repentance? Write the name of the group or individual on the piece of paper you've been given. No one will read it except you. Now pass the pot or bowl around to all participants. Let each person tear up their paper into small pieces and place them in the pot as a sign of releasing judgment over that person or group.

Closing Prayer

Close the session by praying together. First, invite any person who has a prayer request to share it. Ask that individual how the group could best pray for him or her. Next, let one or several people pray for the people they identified on their pieces of paper. Ask God to extend mercy even to those individuals for whom it is difficult for you to pray. Finally, pray for the person on your left, asking that he or she will experience an abundance of God's grace this week.

Between-Sessions
Personal Study

You are invited to further explore the material in this week's study by engaging in any or all of the following activities. Note that these activities are not about following rules or doing your homework. Rather, these activities—action, contemplation, and reflection—are designed to give you an opportunity to be open to God working in your life. Be sure to read the reflection questions after each activity and make a few notes in your study guide about the experience. There will be a time for you to share these reflections at the beginning of the next session.

Action: Paying Attention

During one day this week, pay attention to the way you relate to people who are or seem to be nonbelievers. How do you interact with people who don't know Christ? Are you especially warm to them and look for ways to offer them Christ's love? Or are you more suspicious of them because it's hard for you to trust them? Are you inclined to hurry through your day and not notice them? Do you debate with them or listen to them or ignore them? Make a few notes about your experience to share with the group next week.

Jesus' intention in telling the story was not to impress His hearers with dramatic artistry. Rather, if we understand the parable correctly, its spiritual lessons leave a far more indelible impression on our hearts and minds than any literary analysis of the parable could accomplish. It is therefore of paramount importance to grasp the story's meaning accurately—in its original context and with all the nuances and implications Jesus' original audience would have heard.

JOHN MACARTHUR, *THE PRODIGAL SON*

Contemplation: Reviewing the Passage

For this week's contemplation, review Luke 15:1–10.

¹ *Then all the tax collectors and the sinners drew near to Him to hear Him.* ² *And the Pharisees and scribes complained, saying, "This Man receives sinners and eats with them."* ³ *So He spoke this parable to them, saying:*

⁴ *"What man of you, having a hundred sheep, if he loses one of them, does not leave the ninety-nine in the wilderness, and go after the one which is lost until he finds it?* ⁵ *And when he has found it, he lays it on his shoulders, rejoicing.* ⁶ *And when he comes home, he calls together his friends and neighbors, saying to them, 'Rejoice with me, for I have found my sheep which was lost!'* ⁷ *I say to you that likewise there will be more joy in heaven over one sinner who repents than over ninety-nine just persons who need no repentance.*

⁸ *"Or what woman, having ten silver coins, if she loses one coin, does not light a lamp, sweep the house, and search*

carefully until she finds it? ⁹ And when she has found it, she calls her friends and neighbors together, saying, 'Rejoice with me, for I have found the piece which I lost!' ¹⁰ Likewise, I say to you, there is joy in the presence of the angels of God over one sinner who repents."

Spend some time reviewing the passage you just read, and then consider the following questions:

The words *rejoice* and *joy* are repeated in this passage. What is the significance of the repetition? What is the cause of joy?

When was the last time you participated in that joy?

How could you become a regular participant in that heavenly joy? What personal challenges would you have to overcome in order to do that?

The central imagery is parallel in all three parables. Each parable illustrates the joy of God over the recovery of a lost sinner. Each parable also has a figure representing Christ, whose mission is to seek and to save the lost. In the first parable, the shepherd is symbolic of Christ; in the second, the woman takes that role; and in the Prodigal Son's story, it's the father. (Bear that fact in mind. It is common to assume that the Prodigal's father represents the heavenly Father, but the parallelism of these three stories suggests that he is actually a symbol of Christ.)

JOHN MACARTHUR, *THE PRODIGAL SON*

Reflection: Going Deeper with the Parable

Read the introduction and chapters 1 and 2 in *The Prodigal Son* and reflect on the following questions:

What were some of the faults of the Pharisees? How can you take their example to heart and avoid falling into the same errors?

Jesus never entered into negotiations with the scribes and Pharisees; rather, He stood His ground. Of course, this only heightened the tension, and as a result He was usually at the top of their Most Wanted List. There have been times when many of us have backed down rather than suffer the consequences of standing our ground on what we know to be right. Are there areas of your life where it is easy to negotiate, or compromise, on your convictions? If so, what are those areas, and what have been the results?

Think about your church family and the ways in which you live out your Christian faith. How welcoming are you toward those who are different from you in personality, wealth, ethnicity, social status, cultural background, or physical appearance? On the line below, place an X indicating how willing you believe you are to accept those who are different from you.

Very hesitant or exclusive   Very willing and welcoming

Use the space below to write any key points or questions you want to bring to the next group meeting.

REPENTANCE

Facing the Agony of Being Lost

*Everything about the demand the boy
made cut against the grain of Hebrew
society's core values.*

JOHN MACARTHUR

Jesus began the parable of the two sons with a comment the younger son made to his father: "Father, give me the portion of goods that falls to me" (Luke 15:12). In our culture, the request might seem demanding—even rude—but not all that surprising. We are familiar with a certain sense of entitlement that young people have today, and stories of children being demanding to their parents are certainly not uncommon.

However, to Jesus' first-century Jewish audience, the younger son would have represented the worst kind of sinner they could imagine. Here was a son who flagrantly dishonored not only his father and his family's property but also his very homeland. Everything about the boy's demand would have cut against the grain of that society's core values.

In order to get inside the parable and feel what its first hearers would have felt, we need to understand that honor was everything in that society. This young man heaped shame on himself and his family through his selfishness, and the response would have been even harsher than the shame attacks people sometimes suffer today when others turn against them in social media. Jesus' audience would have felt this young man deserved the worst of what society could dish out in terms of treating him as an outcast.

With this in mind, let's take a look at what this son did to merit being reckoned as "dead" to all decent people.

Opening the Study

Go around the group and invite everyone to answer the following questions:

- How do children show honor to their parents in our culture?

- What are some things in our society to which we feel entitled?

Last week you were invited to participate in the "Between-Sessions Personal Study" section.

- Did you do one of the activities? If so, which one? If not, why not?

- What are some of the things you wrote down in reflection?

- What did you learn by engaging in these activities?

Reading the Word

Read Luke 15:11–19 aloud in the group. Encourage everyone to listen for a fresh insight during the reading. Listen especially for what you learn about the younger son's character.

11 Then He said: "A certain man had two sons. 12 And the younger of them said to his father, 'Father, give me the portion of goods that falls to me.' So he divided to them his livelihood. 13 And not many days after, the younger son gathered all together, journeyed to a far country, and there wasted his possessions with prodigal living. *14 But when he had spent all, there arose a severe famine in that land, and he began to be in want.* *15 Then he went and joined himself to a citizen of that country, and he sent him into his fields to feed swine.* *16 And he would gladly have filled his stomach with the pods that the swine ate, and no one gave him anything.*

17 "But when he came to himself, he said, 'How many of my father's hired servants have bread enough and to spare, and I perish with hunger! 18 I will arise and go to my father, and will say to him, "Father, I have sinned against heaven and before you, 19 and I am no longer worthy to be called your son. Make me like one of your hired servants."'

Turn to the person next to you and take turns sharing your answers to the following questions:

- What was one thing that stood out to you from the reading? In what ways did that represent a new insight?

- What was the younger son's attitude toward his father? Toward his family inheritance?

- The younger son is a living picture of the effects of sin in a person's life. Why do you think so many people find his kind of life so attractive?

Watching the Video

Play the video teaching segment for session 2. As you watch, use the following outline to record any thoughts or concepts that stand out to you.

NOTES

The prodigal son represented the worst kind of sinner imaginable to the first-century Jewish culture in which Jesus and His hearers lived.

No self-respecting son would ask his father for his part of the estate before his father's death. This would be like saying he wished his father was dead.

The son discounted the value of the family estate by selling it quickly and cheaply. He then dishonored his homeland by moving out of Judea and into a Gentile land.

When famine struck, the son was reduced to living with pigs, which were considered unclean creatures in Jewish eyes.

The younger son is a symbol of the sinners who were coming to Jesus and receiving salvation.

The younger son's repentance began when he came to his senses and made a true and accurate assessment of his condition.

The younger son remembered that his father was rich, generous, and loving. He didn't think his father would restore him as a son, but he hoped to be hired as a servant.

The Pharisees would have expected the father to tell his son to go into the village and abase himself for a week—and then maybe he would tell his son how he could earn his way back into the family. That would be the way to uphold the father's honor.

If you see yourself or someone you know in this extreme prodigal, realize we have a loving Father who offers—by grace alone—a full reconciliation. He is glad to take the shameful sinner and make him into a son (or daughter) with all the rights and privileges.

Group Discussion

Take a few minutes with your group members to discuss what you just watched and explore these concepts in Scripture.

1. After watching the video, what is one question you have that you would like to share with the group?

2. Imagine a family farm built up over generations. What would it do to the prosperity of the farm if a third of the land (the elder son received two-thirds) were quickly sold to anyone willing to bid on it? What price was the family in this story paying for the younger son's choices?

3. What are some of the outrageous things the younger son did? Why would each of these have appalled Jesus' hearers?

4. How is our behavior toward God like the younger son's behavior toward his father?

5. What did the son deserve from his father after this behavior? What do we deserve from God after our sinful behavior?

6. How easy is it for you to identify with the younger son in his rebellion and eventual destitution? Why?

7. What do we learn from the younger son about what repentance means?

Opening Up to the Parable

For this activity, each participant will need a blank piece of paper and a pen.

The younger son got to a place of such desperation that he was willing to live with pigs—and he even wished he could digest the carob pods the pigs ate. Today, think about when you have been in such a season of desperation, and then take five minutes on your own to write a letter to God about it. Tell Him honestly how bad it was, or write a prayer of thanksgiving that you have been delivered from that time. Or, if you're in a time of desperation now, write to God whatever is on your mind about your current situation. Afterward, if you feel comfortable doing so, share what you wrote with the group.

Closing Prayer

Close the session by praying together. Invite any person who has a prayer request to share it, and ask how the group could best pray for him or her. Next, pray for the person on your right. If he or she has shared a prayer request, pray for God to meet that need. If not, ask God to have deep and rich mercy on this person and deliver him or her from any current situations where he or she may feel as stuck as living with pigs in a time of famine. Ask God to show everyone in your group anything about which they need to repent. Ask for soft hearts for that conviction.

Between-Sessions
Personal Study

Y ou are invited to further explore the material in this week's study by engaging in any or all of the following activities. Be sure to read the reflection questions after each activity and make a few notes in your study guide about the experience. There will be a time for you to share these reflections at the beginning of the next session.

Action: Showing Gratitude

It's easy to take seasons of well-being for granted if we're not going through a season of famine. However, during such times we need to avoid being self-righteous like the Pharisees, who congratulated themselves for avoiding the pig farm. Instead, we need to be humble and grateful to God, who through His grace drew us to repentance.

So, as an action plan this week, try practicing gratitude. Thank God daily that you're not in the pigsty—not because of your virtue in avoiding it, but because of His magnificent grace in keeping you from it. Look for at least three other things each day for which you're thankful and write them down either on the "Gratitude List" on the next page or in a journal. Over time, you may find that recording what you're grateful for has a pervasive positive effect on your outlook.

GRATITUDE LIST

The young man is a classic illustration of an undisciplined young person who wastes the best part of his life through extravagant self-indulgence and becomes a slave to his own lust and sin. He is a living picture of the course of sin and how it inevitably debases the sinner.

JOHN MACARTHUR, *THE PRODIGAL SON*

Contemplation: Meditating on the Passage

For this week's contemplation, meditate on Luke 15:11–19. (To *meditate* on a passage means to chew on it so that it nourishes you with its deepest truths.)

> [11] *Then He said: "A certain man had two sons.* [12] *And the younger of them said to his father, 'Father, give me the portion of goods that falls to me.' So he divided to them his livelihood.* [13] *And not many days after, the younger son gathered all together, journeyed to a far country, and there wasted his possessions with prodigal living.* [14] *But when he had spent all, there arose a severe famine in that land, and he began to be in want.* [15] *Then he went and joined himself to a citizen of that country, and he sent him into his fields to feed swine.* [16] *And he would gladly have filled his stomach with the pods that the swine ate, and no one gave him anything.*
>
> [17] *"But when he came to himself, he said, 'How many of my father's hired servants have bread enough and to spare, and I perish with hunger!* [18] *I will arise and go to my father, and will say to him, "Father, I have sinned against heaven and before you,* [19] *and I am no longer worthy to be called your son. Make me like one of your hired servants." '*

Choose a word or phrase from this passage that stands out to you and write it down.

You've already studied this passage, so this is an opportunity to let one small piece of it make a deeper impact on your soul. Maybe it's the pods the swine were eating. Maybe it's the phrase "wasted his possessions" or "I will arise and go to my father." Maybe it's the younger son's realization that he had "sinned against heaven." Spend some time mulling over that phrase in your mind, and then consider the following questions:

What is it about that phrase that stands out to you?

What does it contribute to the story as a whole?

What does it tell you about God and the things of God?

What does it tell you about the younger son?

What does it reveal about the process of repentance?

> *Facing the reality of his own circumstances is what caused such a monumental change in the Prodigal's attitude toward his father. Prior to this, he had not showed a hint of respect, affection, or even simple appreciation for his father. Now he was forced to confess that he would be vastly better off at the lowest level of servitude under his own father than far away in the pig fields, reaping the bitter fruits of his "freedom" and literally facing death as a reward for his foolish pursuit of selfish pleasure. He had stupidly spurned his father's jurisdiction when he held the status of a son. He was now perfectly willing to come back under his father's authority as a lowly hired servant. That would by any measure be a major step up from where he was now. Besides, it was the only way out of this mess that was open to him.*
>
> JOHN MACARTHUR, *THE PRODIGAL SON*

Reflection: Going Deeper with the Parable

Read chapters 3 through 6 in *The Prodigal Son* and reflect on the following questions:

What do you learn from these chapters about the younger son's appalling behavior beyond what you learned from the video?

What did you learn about repentance? Why do you think God allows people to rebel against Him?

How did your life before Christ reflect the attitudes of the younger son? Have you ever repented as thoroughly as he did?

In what ways are you sometimes still like the younger son? In what ways are you different from the younger son?

Use the space below to write any key points or questions you want to bring to the next group meeting.

FORGIVENESS

Experiencing Our Father's Love

*The Prodigal therefore hung helpless
in the balance between life and death,
and if his father turned him away,
he would be doomed.*

JOHN MACARTHUR

Today in our culture, it's all too common for a teen or young adult to become a drug addict, steal to support the habit, get in trouble with the law, and make a wreck of his or her life, humiliating the family in the process. However, if the child gets clean and sober—and seeks reconciliation with the family—most parents are overjoyed and not inclined to punish the penitent child more than life has already punished him or her.

Even if the child has lied to and stolen from the parents, they are still generally willing and even eager to take their child back into the family—if that child has truly given up the addiction. People today would be shocked if the family expected the wayward child to make restitution to them for the rest of his or her life for the crime of dishonoring the family. They would be shocked if the family refused to get the needed rehabilitation for the child.

However, in Jesus' day things were very different. Family honor was *everything*, and people would have been shocked if the family *didn't* make the wayward child pay for shaming the family. We need to understand that difference if we are to grasp the outrageousness of the story Jesus was telling to His Jewish audience.

The father of the prodigal son is indeed the hero of the story, but to Jesus' first hearers he would have been considered an unusual and even shameful father.

Opening the Study

Go around the group and invite everyone to answer the following questions:

- What are some of the perceptions that society has about fathers today? Do you feel these are accurate? Why or why not?

- What are some of the ways that parents handle crises in the family today?

Last week you were invited to participate in the "Between-Sessions Personal Study" section.

- Did you do one of the activities? If so, which one? If not, why not?

- What are some of the things you wrote down in reflection?

- What did you learn by engaging in these activities?

Reading the Word

Read Luke 15:20–24 aloud in the group. Encourage everyone to listen for a fresh insight during the reading. Listen especially for what you learn about the father's character.

> [20] *"And he arose and came to his father. But when he was still a great way off, his father saw him and had compassion, and ran and fell on his neck and kissed him. [21] And*

the son said to him, 'Father, I have sinned against heaven and in your sight, and am no longer worthy to be called your son.'

[22] *"But the father said to his servants, 'Bring out the best robe and put it on him, and put a ring on his hand and sandals on his feet.* [23] *And bring the fatted calf here and kill it, and let us eat and be merry;* [24] *for this my son was dead and is alive again; he was lost and is found.' And they began to be merry."*

Turn to the person next to you and take turns sharing your answers to the following questions:

- What was one thing that stood out to you from the reading this time? In what ways did that represent a new insight?

- What do we learn about the father in this passage?

- How is the father depicted like God in these verses?

Watching the Video

Play the video teaching segment for session 3. As you watch, use the following outline to record any thoughts or concepts that stand out to you.

NOTES

In the culture of the day, no father could be as dishonored as the father was in this story.

The standards of Jewish culture said the younger son should try to earn his way back into the family through self-abasement as a hired hand for the rest of his life. He should pay restitution.

The father saw the son a long way off because he was *looking* for him. In the same way, God is looking for the sinner. He is not reluctant when He sees the penitent coming back to Him.

The father had to hike up his robe to run to meet his son, which in that day was considered a shameful act. The father was willing to bear shame to be reconciled with his wayward son.

In the parable, the robe was a symbol of dignity and honor; sandals were a sign of sonship (because slaves went barefoot); and the ring was a sign of authority.

The younger son's *unearned restoration* would have been shocking to the Pharisees.

Jesus is God who came down from glory, humbled Himself, ran through the dusty streets of our world, and took our shame in order to embrace us and make us His sons (and daughters).

God receives sinners for His own joy.

Group Discussion

Take a few minutes with your group members to discuss what you just watched and explore these concepts in Scripture.

1. After watching the video, what is one question you have that you would like to share with the group?

2. How was the father in this story different from what Jesus' original hearers would have expected?

3. Do you think the father condoned his son's sin by his actions? Explain your view.

4. Do you think there was something wrong with this father that made it understandable for his son at first to want to get away from him? How can you tell?

5. The father ran to meet his son instead of waiting for the son to come to him. How is this like God? Why is it important for us to know this about God?

6. Consider what the robe, sandals, and ring represented in the parable. How are these gifts like what God has given us?

7. Describe your experience of God the Father. In what ways have you experienced Him treating you the way the father in this story treated his wayward son? How has your experience affected the way you relate to the Father now?

Opening Up to the Parable

For this activity, each participant will need a blank piece of paper and a pen.

Draw a picture of something from this week's passage that represents what the father has done for you. You could draw sandals, a ring, or the father embracing his son. Drawing engages areas of the brain that talking does not, so try to depict the scene (even if you can only draw stick figures) to let that image sink more deeply into your mind. (If you really don't want to draw, then try describing what you would like to draw.)

Closing Prayer

Close the session by praying together. Invite any person who has a prayer request to share it, and ask how the group could best pray for him or her. Next, pray for the person on your left. If he or she has shared a prayer request, pray for God to meet that need. If not, pray that he or she would deeply experience the Father running and embracing him or her in a real way during the upcoming week.

Between-Sessions
Personal Study

You are invited to further explore the material in this week's study by engaging in any or all of the following activities. Be sure to read the reflection questions after each activity and make a few notes in your study guide about the experience. There will be a time for you to share these reflections at the beginning of the next session.

Action: Being Like the Father

This week, look for an opportunity to be the father in this story for someone else. Whom can you pursue on God's behalf? That person may not yet be repentant, but he or she still needs a taste of the father's grace and love. Try interacting with a non-Christian the way the father in the story would. If there's nothing you can do to welcome that person home yet, try praying and watch for him or her to return from the far country. Let yourself feel what God feels.

This imagery of the father running to meet the Prodigal Son fills in the details of the big picture even more. It illustrates the truth that God is slow to anger and swift to forgive. He has no pleasure in the death of the wicked but is eager, willing, even delighted to save sinners.

JOHN MACARTHUR, *THE PRODIGAL SON*

Contemplation: Meditating on the Passage

For this week's contemplation, meditate on Luke 15:20–24. (Remember that to *meditate* on a passage means to chew on it so that it nourishes you with its deepest truths!)

> [20] *"And he arose and came to his father. But when he was still a great way off, his father saw him and had compassion, and ran and fell on his neck and kissed him.* [21] *And the son said to him, 'Father, I have sinned against heaven and in your sight, and am no longer worthy to be called your son.'*
>
> [22] *"But the father said to his servants, 'Bring out the best robe and put it on him, and put a ring on his hand and sandals on his feet.* [23] *And bring the fatted calf here and kill it, and let us eat and be merry;* [24] *for this my son was dead and is alive again; he was lost and is found.' And they began to be merry."*

Choose a word or phrase from this passage that stands out to you and write it down. What is it about that word or phrase that stands out to you? If the word you chose is something concrete like *robe*, *ring*, or *sandals*, try visualizing that item and what is done with it in the story. Spend some time mulling over in your mind what you have chosen, and then consider the following questions:

What does the word or phrase contribute to the story as a whole?

What does it tell you about God or the things of God?

What does it tell you about the way God welcomes repentant sinners back to Him?

What does it tell you about your relationship with God? How will you respond?

The ceremonial presentation of the three gifts was no mere sentimental gesture. The father was making a public decla-ration that carried profound and far-reaching legal weight. Just as the sandals signified that the Prodigal was to be treated as a son rather than a hired servant, and the robe demonstrated that he was not merely a son but a highly favored one, the signet ring carried a meaning that everyone in that culture understood. It formally endowed the Prodigal Son with a legal right . . . to use someone else's property or assets freely and reap the fruits of them as if they were one's own personal possessions.

JOHN MACARTHUR, *THE PRODIGAL SON*

Reflection: Going Deeper with the Parable

Read chapters 7 and 8 in *The Prodigal Son* and reflect on the following questions:

What did you learn from these chapters about the significance of the father running to meet his son? How does this reflect God's character?

What more thorough understanding of the sandals, robe, and ring did you learn from these chapters? How have you received these things from God?

How do you respond to the honors and privileges the father heaped on his younger son? Do they seem fair to the elder son? Explain.

Why is it important that the father was the one who initiated reconciliation with his son? How has God done the same for you?

Use the space below to write any key points or questions you want to bring to the next group meeting.

PRETENSE

Looking Good Isn't Good Enough

*Of the two types of sinners, the
wanton sinner is much more likely
than the sanctimonious sinner to
face the reality of his own fallenness,
repent, and seek salvation.*

JOHN MACARTHUR

Most parents are satisfied when their children are just obedient to them. They are often less concerned about the reasons *why* their children are obeying. Grudging obedience seems good enough. Approval-seeking obedience is better still. Children who want to show off their performance for reasons of personal pride might be rewarded.

God, however, is more concerned about motivations. He doesn't want us to obey Him merely out of fear or a sense of duty—He wants us to obey Him because we love Him and trust that His will is the best for our lives. God isn't satisfied with performance. He longs for our humility in doing good for the sake of others.

As we have seen throughout this study, the Pharisees—who were among Jesus' listeners—didn't understand this aspect of God. They thought God was pleased with them because of their outstanding performance and good deeds. They also thought they had a *right* to look down on those who had been openly rebellious toward the Father.

It's no wonder, then, that they were completely unprepared for the turn that Jesus' parable was about to take.

Opening the Study

Go around the group and invite everyone to answer the following questions:

- How do children show honor to their parents in our culture?

- What are some things in our society that we feel entitled to have?

Last week you were invited to participate in the "Between-Sessions Personal Study" section.

- Did you do one of the activities? If so, which one? If not, why not?

- What are some of the things you wrote down in reflection?

- What did you learn by engaging in these activities?

Reading the Word

Read Luke 15:25–32 aloud in the group. Invite everyone to listen for a fresh insight during the reading. Listen especially for what you learn about the older son's character.

> ²⁵ *"Now his older son was in the field. And as he came and drew near to the house, he heard music and dancing.* ²⁶ *So he called one of the servants and asked what these things meant.* ²⁷ *And he said to him, 'Your brother has come, and because he has received him safe and sound, your father has killed the fatted calf.'*
> ²⁸ *"But he was angry and would not go in. Therefore his father came out and pleaded with him.* ²⁹ *So he answered and said to his father, 'Lo, these many years I have been*

serving you; I never transgressed your commandment at any time; and yet you never gave me a young goat, that I might make merry with my friends. [30] But as soon as this son of yours came, who has devoured your livelihood with harlots, you killed the fatted calf for him.'

[31] *"And he said to him, 'Son, you are always with me, and all that I have is yours. [32] It was right that we should make merry and be glad, for your brother was dead and is alive again, and was lost and is found.'"*

Turn to the person next to you and take turns sharing your answers to the following questions:

- What was one thing that stood out to you from the reading? In what ways did that represent a new insight?

- Why was the elder son angry? Do you think he had a right to be angry? Why or why not?

- What did the elder son fail to understand about the relationship his father wanted to have with him?

Watching the Video

Play the video teaching segment for session 4. As you watch, use the following outline to record any thoughts or concepts that stand out to you.

NOTES

In this parable, Jesus was illustrating two kinds of sinners. The first was openly rebellious and blatantly sinful, showing disdain for his father and family. The second was a secretive sinner, hiding his sin, wanting to be thought of as moral, religious, and spiritual.

The older brother hid his hatred for his father and brother under the cloak of good works. As far as the community was concerned, he was the good son. But he was no less a sinner.

Where was the older son at the beginning of the story, when his younger brother was making disastrous choices and dishonoring his father? He didn't try to protect his brother or his father. He was absent because he had no relationship with either of them.

The elder son came in from the field, where he had been doing his duty grudgingly. He heard about the party and became angry at his father's forgiveness. He had no category for grace.

Jesus told this story to the scribes and Pharisees, who were angry at Him for offering forgiveness to blatant sinners.

Religious people are resistant to the only thing that can save them: grace. Religion is usually more damning than outright rebellion. But God offers forgiveness to both kinds of sinners. He does it for His own joy.

Group Discussion

Take a few minutes with your group members to discuss what you just watched and explore these concepts in Scripture.

1. After watching the video, what is one question you have that you would like to share with the group?

2. In what ways can you identify with the elder son in this story?

3. What were the scribes and Pharisees invited to learn from this part of the parable?

4. How can we tell from the story that the elder son secretly hated his father?

5. When the father said, "Son, you are always with me, and all that I have is yours" (verse 31), what did that say about the way Jesus viewed the Pharisees?

6. Why do you think it was so hard for the scribes and Pharisees to celebrate the repentance of notorious sinners?

7. Why do you think religious people are often so resistant to seeking forgiveness and receiving grace for themselves?

Opening Up to the Parable

For this activity, each participant will need a blank piece of paper and a pen.

On your own, with no one looking, write a letter to God about your temptation toward one of the two types of sin discussed in this session: (1) blatant rebellion, which doesn't care what people think; or (2) secretive sin, which wants to be thought of as moral and spiritual. Consider which of these has tempted you the most in the past, which tempts you now, and what grace you need from God to turn your back on these tendencies.

Closing Prayer

Close the session by praying together. Invite any person who has a prayer request to share it, and ask how the group could best pray for him or her. As a group, pray for those specific requests, and also pray that God would deliver each of the group members from secretive sin. Ask God to help you care about the openly sinful people around you and to help you rejoice when they come to their senses and repent. Also pray to become aware of and free from insidious self-righteousness and pride. Implore God to deliver you from blindness to your own faults. Finally, spend some time thanking Him that He is eager to restore relationship with any kind of sinner and that He loves each member of your group.

BETWEEN-SESSIONS PERSONAL STUDY

You are invited to further explore the material in this week's study by engaging in any or all of the following activities. Be sure to read the reflection questions after each activity and make a few notes in your study guide about the experience. There will be a time for you to share these reflections at the beginning of the next session.

Action: Sharing Your Desires with God

The elder son had built up resentment against his father. He complained, "You never gave me a young goat, that I might make merry with my friends" (verse 29). He clearly had desires for things he wanted from his father that he had never told his father about. He may not have even articulated those desires to himself before they burst out of his mouth in anger.

Spend some time talking with God about your desires. You might want to do this with pen and paper, putting the words down where you can see them. What have you longed to get from God that you don't have? Do you have any resentment or disappointment about things you want from God but haven't received? If so, tell Him the whole story. Everything He has is yours, and if there is something you have asked for repeatedly but haven't received, He has His reasons for the timing. And it may be that He is waiting for you to ask openly and persistently!

The elder son is the third major character in the parable, and as it turns out, he is the one who embodies the parable's main lesson. His most obvious characteristic is his resentment for his younger brother. But underneath that, and even more ominously, it is clear that he has been nurturing a quietly smoldering hatred for the father—for a long, long time, it appears. This secretly rebellious spirit has shaped and molded his character in a most disturbing way.

JOHN MACARTHUR, *THE PRODIGAL SON*

Contemplation: Meditating on the Passage

For this week's contemplation, meditate on Jesus' words in Luke 15:25–32:

²⁵ *"Now his older son was in the field. And as he came and drew near to the house, he heard music and dancing.* ²⁶ *So he called one of the servants and asked what these things meant.* ²⁷ *And he said to him, 'Your brother has come, and because he has received him safe and sound, your father has killed the fatted calf.'*

²⁸ *"But he was angry and would not go in. Therefore his father came out and pleaded with him.* ²⁹ *So he answered and said to his father, 'Lo, these many years I have been serving you; I never transgressed your commandment at*

any time; and yet you never gave me a young goat, that I might make merry with my friends. ³⁰ But as soon as this son of yours came, who has devoured your livelihood with harlots, you killed the fatted calf for him.'

³¹ "And he said to him, 'Son, you are always with me, and all that I have is yours. ³² It was right that we should make merry and be glad, for your brother was dead and is alive again, and was lost and is found.'"

Just as you have done in previous weeks during this study, choose one particular word or phrase in this passage that stands out to you. Pay particular attention to what the older son is doing when the party for the younger son starts, how he reacts to his father, and how the father responds to him. Write down the word or phrase, spend some time mulling it over in your mind, and then consider the following questions:

What is it about that word or phrase that stands out to you?

What does it contribute to the story as a whole?

What does it tell you about the attitude and actions of the older son?

What does it reveal about God's grace toward all kinds of sinners?

The Prodigal's brother gives us a vivid depiction of how the Pharisees saw things. He illustrates why they were so haughty and hateful in their dealings with others. They disdained the idea that divine grace was sufficient to save sinners. They resented the mercy of immediate forgiveness. They scoffed at Jesus' teaching that sinners could be justified by faith and instantly reconciled with the heavenly Father.

JOHN MACARTHUR, *THE PRODIGAL SON*

Reflection: Going Deeper with the Parable

Read chapters 9 and 10 in *The Prodigal Son* and reflect on the following questions:

What additional information do you learn about the elder son after reading these chapters?

How was the elder son's sin like his brother's sin? How was it different?

How could the elder brother have received forgiveness and grace?

Read Matthew 21:28–32. What point is Jesus making in this parable? How is it parallel to the parable that He told of the prodigal son?

What, if anything, do these chapters say about *you*?

Use the space below to write any key points or questions you want to bring to the next group meeting.

GRACE

Receiving Our Most Amazing Gift

*The abruptness of the ending doesn't
leave us without the point . . . it is
the point.*

JOHN MACARTHUR

Imagine a retelling of the classic children's tale *Cinderella* in which the story ends with the prince looking everywhere for the owner of the glass slipper, but never finding her. There would be no resolution to the fairy tale—just an ongoing search. We would never find out if the prince's quest ultimately ends in sorrow or in joy.

Yet that's the kind of cliffhanger we have in the parable of the prodigal son. The story ends with the father pleading with his elder son to be reconciled to his brother and to join the celebration. There is no resolution. We never find out if the older son puts aside his anger and goes to the party, escalates the conflict by pressing his complaints, or does something else.

Why? Why does Jesus, a master storyteller, leave us hanging?

Opening the Study

Go around the group and invite everyone to answer the following questions:

- What is your definition of grace? What does it look like in your life?

- Why do you think some people have trouble accepting God's grace to others—and perhaps even to themselves?

Last week you were invited to participate in the "Between-Sessions Personal Study" section.

- Did you do one of the activities? If so, which one? If not, why not?

- What are some of the things you wrote down in reflection?

- What did you learn by engaging in these activities?

Reading the Word

Read Isaiah 53:4–6 aloud in the group. In this prophecy, God tells His people about the nature of the coming Messiah who will take away the sin of the world. Invite everyone to listen for a fresh insight during the reading.

> ⁴ *Surely He has borne our griefs*
>   *And carried our sorrows;*
> *Yet we esteemed Him stricken,*
>   *Smitten by God, and afflicted.*
> ⁵ *But He was wounded for our transgressions,*
> *He was bruised for our iniquities;*
> *The chastisement for our peace was upon Him,*
>   *And by His stripes we are healed.*
> ⁶ *All we like sheep have gone astray;*
>   *We have turned, every one, to his own way;*
> *And the Lord has laid on Him the iniquity of us all.*

Turn to the person next to you and take turns sharing your answers to the following questions:

- What was one thing that stood out to you from the reading? In what ways did that represent a new insight?

- What does this passage foretell about what Jesus would accomplish on the cross?

- What invitation does this passage offer to people who, like the prodigal son, know they are sinners?

Watching the Video

Play the video teaching segment for session 5. As you watch, use the following outline to record any thoughts or concepts that stand out to you.

NOTES

The older brother had no relationship with his father or his brother. He was furious when he heard that his father had thrown a party for his younger brother. The father pleaded with him to be reconciled. What happens next?

The story ends without telling us what happened to the older brother.

In an oral culture as in Jesus' day, a speaker told stories in parallel stanzas to help in memorizing it. This story has eight stanzas about the father's relationship with the younger son, but only seven stanzas about his relationship with his older son. The final stanza is missing.

What was the response of the older son? One ending would be about the older son's repentance and reconciliation with his father and brother. But that's not what happened.

The real ending would say that the older son was so angry that he picked up a piece of wood and beat his father to death. That's essentially how the

Pharisees really responded to Jesus: they pursued him to death.

Yet in the death of Jesus is the very act of God paying the full penalty for our sins.

Whether we are like the prodigal or like the hypocritical older brother, the gospel of grace is offered to us. The provision for our sin has been made and the price paid in full by Christ.

Group Discussion

Take a few minutes with your group members to discuss what you just watched and explore these concepts in Scripture.

1. After watching the video, what is one question you have that you would like to share with the group?

2. Why didn't Jesus end the story with an account of the elder brother's response to his father?

3. When you consider the father's appeal to his elder son in Luke 15:31–32, what thoughts come to mind?

4. How do you respond to the idea of ending the story with the elder son beating his father to death? Would that be an appropriate ending? Why or why not?

5. What alternatives to killing Jesus did the scribes and Pharisees have?

6. Jesus was indeed killed, but His story didn't end there. He rose, just as He said He would. He later ascended into heaven, where He now sits at the right hand of His Father. How does this reality affect your daily life?

7. What are your most memorable takeaways from this study of the parable of the prodigal son?

Opening Up to the Parable

For this activity, each participant will need a blank piece of paper and a pen.

Sing or play a recording of a song about Jesus' sacrifice at the cross and what it accomplished. Afterward, write letters to God, thanking Him for what He did for you through Jesus' sacrifice. Be as detailed as possible about what He did and why you are grateful to God for it. When you are finished, you may share what you wrote with the group or keep it private.

Closing Prayer

Close this final session in this study by praying together. Invite any person who has a prayer request to share it, and ask how the group could best pray for him or her. During your prayer time as a group, thank God for what you have received from this study. Thank Him also for what your group has meant to you, for sending Jesus as a sacrifice for your sins, and for offering you grace when you most needed it. The letter you wrote to God may offer you some words to articulate your thoughts in prayer.

PERSONAL STUDY FOR THE COMING DAYS

Further explore the good news of the parable of the prodigal son by engaging in any or all of the following activities. Be sure to read the reflection questions after each activity and make a few notes in your study guide about the experience. Consider sharing your reflections in the days ahead with a fellow group member or a close friend.

Action: Getting a Visual

Search an art book or the Internet for a painting depicting the parable of the prodigal son and the crucifixion. (For example, Rembrandt's painting *Prodigal Son* depicts the moment when the father met the prodigal and embraced him.) When you find an image that speaks to you, spend some time studying it and then respond to the questions below.

What does the image convey about the father? About the son?

What do the details—such as the prodigal's appearance and attire—tell you?

What can you learn by placing such a painting side by side with one of the crucifixion? How are the two scenes related?

What images of the crucifixion make the most impact on you? Why?

Of all the surprising plot twists and startling details, this is the culminating surprise: Jesus marvelously shaped the point and then simply walked away without resolving the tension between the father and his firstborn. But there is no missing fragment. He intentionally left the story unfinished and the dilemma unsettled. It is supposed to make us feel like we're waiting for a punch line or final sentence.

JOHN MACARTHUR, THE PRODIGAL SON

Contemplation: Meditating on the Passage

For this week's contemplation, meditate on Isaiah 53:4–6.

> [4] *Surely He has borne our griefs*
> *And carried our sorrows;*
> *Yet we esteemed Him stricken,*
> *Smitten by God, and afflicted.*
> [5] *But He was wounded for our transgressions,*
> *He was bruised for our iniquities;*
> *The chastisement for our peace was upon Him,*
> *And by His stripes we are healed.*
> [6] *All we like sheep have gone astray;*
> *We have turned, every one, to his own way;*
> *And the Lord has laid on Him the iniquity of us all.*

Choose a word or phrase from this passage that stands out to you, write it below, and spend some time mulling over that phrase in your mind. Then consider the following questions:

What is it about that word or phrase that stands out?

What does it contribute to the prophecy as a whole?

What does your word or phrase tell you about Jesus Christ?

What does it say about you? How will you respond?

> Don't forget that Jesus told this parable—including the abrupt ending—chiefly for the benefit of the scribes and Pharisees. It was really a story about them. The elder brother represented them. The hanging resolution underscored the truth that the next move was theirs. The father's final tender plea was Jesus' own gentle appeal to them. If they had demanded to know the end of the parable on the spot, Jesus might well have said to them, "That is up to you." The Pharisees' ultimate response to Jesus would write the end of the story in real life.
>
> JOHN MACARTHUR, *THE PRODIGAL SON*

Reflection: Going Deeper with the Parable

Read chapter 11 in *The Prodigal Son* and reflect on the following questions:

What important insights do you gain from studying the structure of the parable?

How do you react to the Pharisees' ultimate response to Jesus as told in the Gospels? What does it make you do or want to do?

What has Jesus' death and resurrection accomplished for you?

With whom can you share what you've learned from the parable of the prodigal son?

The invitation to be part of the great celebratory banquet is still open to all. It extends even to you, dear reader. And it doesn't matter whether you are an open sinner like the Prodigal Son, a secret one like his elder brother, or someone with characteristics from each type. If you are someone who is still estranged from God, Christ urges you to acknowledge your guilt, admit your own spiritual poverty, embrace your heavenly Father, and be reconciled to Him.

JOHN MACARTHUR, *THE PRODIGAL SON*

ADDITIONAL
RESOURCES
FOR GROUP LEADERS

If you are reading this, you have agreed to lead a group through this study of the parable of the prodigal son. Thank you! What you have chosen to do is important, and much good fruit can come from studies like this one. Thank you for sharing your time and talent.

The five sessions in this study have been built around video content and small group interaction. That's where you come in. As the group leader, you are invited to see yourself as the host of a dinner party. Your job is to take care of your guests by managing all the behind-the-scenes details so that when everyone finally arrives, they can just enjoy one another.

As the group leader, your role is not to answer all the questions or reteach the content—the video, book, and study guide will do most of that work. Your job is to guide the experience and cultivate your small group into a kind of teaching community. This will make it a place to process, question, and reflect—not merely receive more instruction.

As such, make sure everyone in the group gets a copy of the study guide. Group members should feel free to write in their guide and bring it with them every week. This will keep everyone on the same page and help the process run more smoothly. Likewise, encourage each participant (or couple) to get a copy of *The Prodigal Son* book so they can complete the suggested readings in the between-sessions personal study, should they so desire.

If this is not possible, see if anyone from the group is willing to donate an extra copy or two for sharing. Or contact your church to see if they would be open to purchasing some extra copies for your group members. Giving everyone access to all the material will position this study to be as rewarding an experience as possible.

Hosting the Group

As the group leader, you will want to create an environment that is conducive to sharing and learning. For this reason, a church sanctuary or formal classroom may not be ideal, as these spaces can feel formal and less intimate. Whatever space you choose, make sure there is enough comfortable seating for everyone and, if possible, arrange the seats in a semicircle so everyone can easily see the video. This will make transition between the video and group conversation more efficient and natural.

Try to get to the meeting site early (if it is not being held in your home) so you can greet participants as they arrive. Having some simple refreshments available will create a welcoming atmosphere and can be a wonderful addition to a group study event. If you do serve food, try to take into account any food allergies or dietary restrictions your group may have. Also, if you meet in a home, you will want to find out if the house has pets (in case there are any allergies), and even consider offering child care to couples with children who want to attend.

Finally, be sure your media technology is working properly. Managing these details up front will make the rest of your group experience flow more effectively. It will also provide a more welcoming space in which to engage the content of *The Prodigal Son*.

Leading Your Group

Once everyone has arrived, it will be time to begin the group. If you are new to small group leading, what follows are some simple tips to make your group time healthy, enjoyable, and effective. First, consider beginning the meeting with a word of prayer, and then remind people to silence and put away their mobile phones. This is a way for them to say "yes" to being present to one another and to God.

Next, invite someone to read the questions from the "Opening the Study" section in the guide. These will serve as "icebreaker" questions to get the group members interacting and will introduce them to the theme of that week's content. After this time, your group will engage in a simple Bible study called "Reading the Word." Note that you do not need to be a biblical scholar to effectively lead this group time! Your role is only to open up conversation by using the instructions provided and inviting the group into the text.

Now that the group is fully engaged, it is time to watch the video. The content of each session is inspiring and challenging, and there are prompts provided in the guide to help the participants know the key points and take notes. This will serve as some built-in time for personal reflection before anyone in the group is asked to respond to the content. Internal processors will find this time helpful to sort through their thoughts and questions, and it will make the group discussion time more fruitful.

During the group discussion, encourage everyone to participate, but make sure each person knows he or she does not have to do so. As the discussion progresses, follow up with comments such as, "Tell me more about that," or "Why did you answer the way you did?" This will allow participants to deepen their reflections and will invite meaningful sharing in a nonthreatening way.

You have been given multiple questions to use in each session. You do not have to use them all or follow them in order. Feel free to pick and choose questions based on either the needs of your group or how the conversation is flowing. Adapt the content as needed to fit the dynamics of your group. Also, don't be afraid of silence. Offering a question and allowing up to thirty seconds of silence is okay. It allows people space and time to think about how they want to respond.

As group leader, you are the boundary keeper for your group. Do not let anyone (yourself included) dominate the group time. Keep an eye out for group members who might be tempted to attack folks they disagree with or try to fix those having struggles. These kinds of behaviors can derail a group's momentum, so they need to be shut down. Model "active listening" and encourage everyone in your group to do the same. This will make your group time a safe space and foster the kind of community that God can use to change people.

The group discussion time leads to the final and most dynamic part of this study, "Opening Up to the Parable." During this section participants are invited to transform what they have learned into practical action. Take some time to read over this section ahead of time so you can be prepared on how to lead your group through the experience.

Finally, even though there are instructions for how to conclude each session in prayer, feel free to strike out on your own. Just make sure you do something intentional to mark the end of the meeting. It may also be helpful to take time before or after the closing prayer to go over that week's between-sessions personal study. This will allow people to consider the material and ask any questions they might have so everyone can depart in confidence.

Debriefing the Between-Sessions Materials

As mentioned, each week there is between-sessions work where everyone is invited to do some additional reading, study, and reflection on the key points of the parable. Your job at the beginning of the current week's session is to help the group members debrief the previous week's experience. Beginning in session 2, this will take place during the "Opening the Study" section, right after the icebreaker questions.

Debriefing something like this is a bit different from responding to questions based on the video because the content comes from the participants' real lives. The basic items that you want the group to reflect on are: (1) *What was my takeaway from the activities I did?* (2) *What was the hardest thing I did?* (3) *What did I learn about myself?* and (4) *What did I learn about God?*